warm
hands
warm *the* heart™

44139001006786

Edited by Kara Gott Warner

HOUSE of
WHITE
BIRCHES

PUBLISHERS
SINCE 1947

Table of Contents

Bracknell Forest Borough Council

3162676

Askews & Holts	2011

Introduction

If you're new to mitten making, this book will introduce you to a world of exciting projects and techniques. In the pages to follow, you'll discover four different knitting methods for creating your mittens. As you learn and adapt to these methods, you may find that you favor working in one style over another.

The Methods:

1. Working on double-point needles

2. Working on two circular needles

3. Using the Magic loop method on one circular needle

4. Working back and forth using straight needles

You'll also learn how to apply the following four stitch and color combinations to your knitted creations that will add interest and excitement to your mittens:

1. Fair Isle

2. Intarsia

3. Twining

4. Drop Stitch

Once you master these useful techniques, you'll be inspired time and time again to "share the love" and make mittens for all those special gift-giving occasions.

Kara

Kara Gott Warner, Editor

Circular Knitting Techniques

Work in Working With Double-Point Needles (dpn)

Double-points come in sets of five and are usually European made. With these, the work is divided evenly among three or four needles, with the fourth or fifth being 6-9 inches. Very short (4-inch) needles are available from specialty sources and are often know as glove or finger needles. These are especially useful when working thumbs.

If you are new to working with double-points, it may feel awkward at first. This is normal and, as with any new endeavor, will go away with time as you become more comfortable manipulating multiple needles.

Casting on

Cast on one-third the desired number of stitches onto the first needle. Holding the second needle parallel and below the first, cast on another one-third of the stitches. Hold the third needle parallel below the first two and cast on the remaining one-third. Photo 1 shows 10 stitches cast onto each needle. Tip: If you prefer, you can also cast on all of your stitches onto a straight needle, then transfer the stitches to each separate double-point needle.

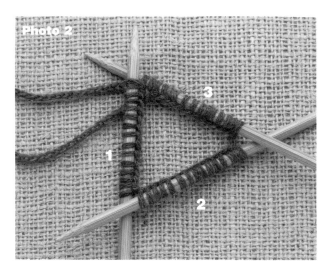

Photo 2

Arranging the Needles

Rearrange the needles to form a triangle, with the base closest to you and the point facing away. All the stitches are at the bottom of the needles and should not be twisted. Both the tail end and the end of yarn connected to the skein are at the left end of needle 3 (see photo 2). If you're using four needles, rearrange the needles to form a square so that the tail end and the end of yarn connected to the skein are at the left end of needle 4.

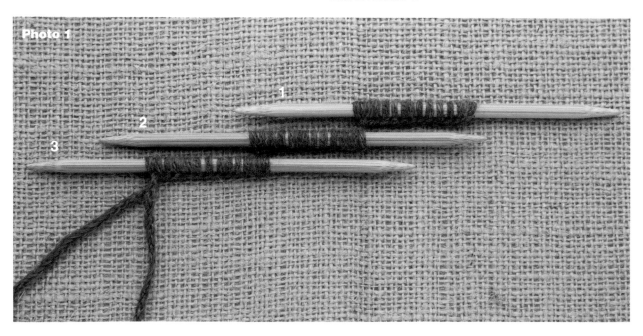

Photo 1

Slip the first stitch from needle 1 and place onto needle 3. Slip the ending stitch from needle 3 up and over the stitch just transferred onto needle 1 to "join" into a ring.

Using the end of yarn connected to the skein and the fourth (free) needle, knit the stitches on the first needle. When all stitches are on the new needle, the needle that formerly held the stitches now becomes the free needle. Continue turning the work, so you are always working at the "base" of the triangle. The yarn tail will mark the beginning of needle 1. To avoid a "ladder" of larger stitches from forming when you change from one needle to the next, work the first stitch of each needle a bit tighter than usual.

Photo 3 shows a cuff being worked in K1, P1 ribbing. Our sample of 30 stitches works out rather nicely with 10 stitches per needle. In K1, P1 ribbing, this means there will always be a starting needle with a knit, and ending with a purl, exactly even with the pattern.

Photo 3

But what about a cuff with 32 stitches worked in K2, P2 rib? Dividing by three doesn't work out evenly. We could put 11 stitches on each of the first two needles and 10 on the last, which translates beginning needle 1 with K2 and end with P1. Needle 2 would begin with P1 and end with K2, while needle 3 would begin and end with P2, making it hard to develop a knitting rhythm, but easy to make a mistake. The solution is to rearrange the stitches so we have 12 stitches each on the first and last needles, and eight on the second. With all number being multiples of four, you can work around the cuff in K2, P2 ribbing always coming out even.

Working With Two Circular Needles

Cast on the required number of stitches onto a circular needle. Slip half of the stitches to a second circular needle. Needle 1 holds the first group of stitches and needle 2 holds the rest of the stitches.

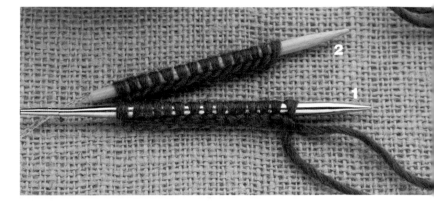

Step 1: Slide all stitches to other end of needles, making sure that needle 2 is on top, and needle 1 is on the bottom.

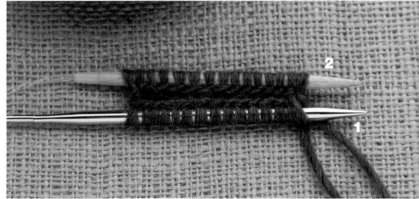

Step 2: Slip the first stitch from needle 1 and place onto needle 2. Slip the ending stitch from needle 2 up and over the stitch just transferred onto needle 1 to "join" into a ring.

Needle 1 Cable

Step 3: Pull needle 1 so the stitches rest on the cable.

Step 4: The working yarn is on needle 2, ready to work. Pick up the other end of needle 2 and work across all stitches.

Step 5: Turn the work so needle 1 is ready to work. Pull needle 2 so stitches rest on cable. Pick up opposite end of needle 1 and work across all stitches.

Continue in this manner until desired length is reached.

Using Magic Loop Method

This method of working in the round uses one long circular needle, ideally one with a very flexible cable. It is very similar to working with two circular needles but many knitters prefer it to working with two needles because it eliminates the distracting loose ends of the second circular needle. Once you master this technique, it's a great solution when working on small-circumference projects.

Cast on or pick up the required number of stitches onto a 29-inch, or longer, circular needle. Slide the stitches to the cable portion of the needle. Pinch the cable in half as shown below, then pull to create a large loop. Arrange half the stitches on one needle tip, and half on the other.

Follow these 3 easy steps:

Step 1: The photo below shows how your stitches should look after you have distributed them on the two parts of the needle. The points of the needle and the "tail" from the cast on row are facing to the right and the cables are on your left.

Tip: *After cast on row: refer to Working with Two Circular Needles to join the first and last stitch.*

Step 2: The next step, as shown below illustrates how to begin working your first round: Hold the needle in your left hand, and pull out the needle that holds the "tail end"; the stitches that were on the needle point are now resting on the cable. Begin working the stitches that are still on the opposite needle point as if you were working on straight needles.

Step 3: At the end of the row, simply turn the work around and reposition the stitches as shown. Once again, the needles are pointing to the right, and the cable loop is to the left.

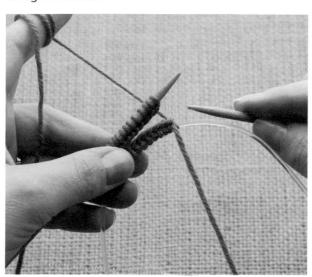

Continue to work in this manner until desired length is reached.

The example below shows how the work will appear on the needle as the work gets longer.

Moulin Rouge

These sultry gauntlets are luxurious, super-soft and simply stunning.

Design by Lisa Ellis

Skill Level

■■■□ INTERMEDIATE

Size

Woman's small/medium

Finished Measurements

Hand circumference: 6 inches
Length: 12 inches

Materials

- Cascade Yarns Cloud 9 (worsted weight; 50% merino wool/ 50% angora; 109 yds/50g per ball): 1 ball each red #146 (A) and black #120 (B)
- Two size 8 (5mm) 16-inch circular needles or size needed to obtain gauge
- Two size 9 (5.5mm) 16-inch circular needles or size needed to obtain gauge
- 1 locking stitch marker

Gauge

22 sts and 20 rnds = 4 inches/10cm in Twined St with smaller needles.

19 sts and 20 rnds = 4 inches/10cm in Twined St with larger needles.

To save time, take time to check gauge.

Special Abbreviation

Knit in front and back of stitch (kfb): Increase made by knitting in front loop, then back loop of same stitch.

Pattern Stitch

Twined Knitting (multiple of 2 sts)

Rnd 1: *K1A, k1B; rep from * around, always bringing the new yarn up over the top of old yarn.
Rnd 2: *K1B, k1A; rep from * around, always bringing the new yarn up over the top of the old yarn.

Rep Rnds 1 and 2 for pat and untwist yarns frequently.

Special Techniques

Elastic Bind-Off: [*Wyib, sl 1p, bring yarn forward between needles, move slipped st back to LH needle, bring yarn to back of work between needles, k1; rep from * once more, pass first st over 2nd and off needle to bind off 1] to end.

Sideways Trim: Bring both yarns to front of work. *P1B over A, and p1A over B; rep from * around, always bringing the new yarn up over the top of old yarn.

Pattern Notes

These fingerless gloves are worked from the cuff up, using 2 short circular needles.

To keep stitches from lining up at the beginning of the round while working the Twined pattern a stitch is added after completing the Sideways Trim round.

The wrist shaping is achieved by changing to one size smaller needles. For a more fitted wrist, try using needles two sizes smaller rather than one size smaller than the larger needle.

Refer to Twined Knitting Techniques on page 46 for more information on this method of two-color knitting.

Left Glove

Cuff

With larger needle and A, cast on 40 sts. Distribute sts evenly on 2 circular needles. Place locking marker in edge for beg of rnd and join, taking care not to twist sts.

Next rnd: [K1, p1] around.

Attach B.

Next rnd: [K1A, k1B] around.

Next rnd: Work Sideways Trim.

Note: When working inc, knit in front of st with B and make inc in back with A.

Inc rnd: Work Rnd 1 of Twined St to last st, kfb—41 sts.

Work in Twined Knitting, continue from Rnd 2 until glove measures 6 inches from beg.

Wrist
Change to smaller needles.

Continue in established pat until glove measures 10½ inches from beg.

Hand
Change to larger needles and work in established pat to last 6 sts, place next 12 sts onto waste yarn for thumb—29 sts.

Move locking marker to next st for beg of rnd and join.

Next rnd: Work in established pat around, pulling first st firmly over thumb opening.

Work 5 more rnds in established pat.

Next rnd: Work Sideways Trim. Cut B.

Next rnd: With A only, [k1, p1] around, making sure to knit B sts and purl A sts.

Bind off in Elastic Bind-Off.

Thumb
Place sts from waste yarn on larger needles, with first 6 sts on one needle and rem 6 sts on 2nd needle.

Attach A and B, pick up 1 st in top of opening with same color as next st, work in next rnd of Twined Knitting to end, pick up 1 st in top of opening with next color—14 sts.

Work in established pat for 4 more rnds.

Next rnd: Work Sideways Trim. Cut B.

Next rnd: With A only, [k1, p1] around, making sure to knit B sts and purl A sts.

Bind off in Elastic Bind-Off.

Right Glove
Work same as for left glove.

Finishing
Block to finished measurements. ●

Celtic Moors

These color-stranded mittens will keep you extra warm throughout the winter months.

Design by Jeannette Ehrich

. . . .

Skill Level
■■■■▷ EXPERIENCED

Sizes
Adult small/medium (medium/large)
Instructions are given for the smaller size, with larger size in parentheses. When only 1 number is given, it applies to both sizes.

Finished Measurements
Hand circumference: 8¼ (8¾) inches
Length: 9½ (10¾) inches

Materials
- Mission Falls 136 Merino Superwash (DK weight; 100% merino wool; 136 yds/50g per ball): 2 (2) balls raisin #012 (MC) and 1 (2) ball(s) curry #013 (CC)

  3 LIGHT
- Size 2 (2.75mm) double-point needles (set of 4)
- Size 4 (3.5mm) double-point needles (set of 4) or size needed to obtain gauge
- Stitch markers

Gauge
30 sts and 30 rows = 4 inches/10cm in Ram's Horn pat with larger needles.

To save time, take time to check gauge.

Special Abbreviations
Make 1 (M1): Increase by making a backward loop over RH needle.

Make 1 Left (M1L): Insert LH needle from front to back under strand between the last st worked and the next st on LH needle, k1-tbl. St slants to the left.

Make 1 Right (M1R): Insert LH needle from back to front under strand between the last st worked and

the next st on LH needle, k1 through front of loop. St slants to the right.

N1, N2, N3: Needle 1, Needle 2, Needle 3.

Pattern Stitch
Celtic Moors

Refer to Celtic Moors chart on pages 15 and 16.

Special Technique
Two Color Cast-On: Make a slip knot on needle with both yarns held tog and MC to right (these loops do not count as sts), leaving tails about 4 inches. Holding both yarns as you would for a long tail cast-on, with the MC over your thumb and the CC over your index finger, cast on the required number of sts. Slide the slip knot off and gently pull the ends to tighten the first st.

Left Mitten

Cuff
With smaller needles, cast on 54 (57) sts using the Two-Color Cast-On. Distribute sts evenly on 3 needles—18 (19) sts on each needle. Place marker for beg of rnd and join, taking care not to twist sts.

Next rnd: [K2 MC, p1 CC] around.

Continue in established pat until cuff measures 2½ inches.

Thumb gusset
Change to larger needles and CC.

Set-up rnd: [K7, M1] 2 (8) times, [k8, M1] 4 (0) times, [k7, M1] 1 (0) time(s), k1—61 (65) sts.

Distribute sts on needles as follows: N1: 31 (33) sts; N2: 15 (16) sts; N3: 15 (16) sts.

Next rnd: Work Rnd 1 of Hand chart to last 6 sts, place marker, work Rnd 1 of Thumb Gusset chart over next 5 sts, place marker, work last st in Hand chart.

Inc rnd: Work in pat to marker, M1R CC, work in pat to marker, M1L MC, work last st in pat—63 (67) sts.

Rep inc rnd [every other rnd] 4 more times—71 (75) sts.

Work even in pat for 6 (8) rnds.

Hand
Next rnd: Work in pat to marker, slip next 15 sts to waste yarn for thumb, cast on 5 sts in pat, work last st in pat—61 (65) sts.

Continuing in established pat, work through Rnd 42 (50) of chart.

Shape top
Rnd 43 (51): N1: K1 CC, ssk MC, work to last 3 sts on needle, k2tog MC, k1 CC; N2: ssk MC (CC), work to 2 sts before end of chart, k2tog MC—57 (61) sts.

Rnds 44 (52)–50 (57): Continuing in pat, work dec as indicated on chart [every other rnd] twice more, then [every rnd] 3 times, working N1 dec in MC, and maintaining established pat on N2 and N3—37 (41) sts.

Rnd 51 (58): N1: K1 CC, ssk MC, k2tog MC, work to last 5 sts on needle, ssk MC, k2tog MC, k1 CC; N2: ssk MC (CC), work to last 2 sts on needle, k2tog CC (MC); N3: ssk CC, work to last 2 sts on needle, k2tog CC—29 (33) sts.

Rep last dec rnd 2 (1) more time(s), working N1 dec in colors according to chart, and maintaining stripe sequence on N2 and N3—13 (25) sts.

Medium/large size only

Next rnd: K1 CC, ssk MC, k2tog CC, s2kp2 MC, ssk CC, k2tog MC, k1 CC, ssk CC, k2 MC, k2tog CC, ssk MC, k2 CC, k2tog MC—15 sts.

Cut yarn, draw CC to WS and MC through rem sts.

Thumb
Attach yarns and return thumb gusset sts to larger needles as follows: N1: Beg at palm side of gusset and, pick up and knit 2 sts in pat, work first 6 sts from thumb gusset in established pat; N2: work next 8 sts in established pat; N3: work rem st, pick up and knit 2 sts at corner of opening, and pick up and knit 5 sts in pat along cast-on edge at top of opening—24 sts. Place marker for beg of rnd and join.

Work in established pat until thumb measures 2¼ (2½) inches, or approx ¼ inch less than desired length.

Shape top
Rnd 1: *Ssk in pat, to last 2 sts on N1, k2tog in pat; rep from * across N2 and N3—18 sts.

Work 1 rnd even.

Rnd 3: Rep [Rnd 1]—12 sts.

Cut yarn and draw CC to WS and MC through rem sts.

Right Mitten

Cuff
Work same as left cuff.

Thumb gusset
Change to larger needles and CC.

Set-up rnd: [K7, M1] 2 (8) times, [k8, M1] 4 (0) times, [k7, M1] 1 (0) time(s), k1—61 (65) sts.

Distribute sts on needles as follows: N1: 31 (33) sts; N2: 15 (16) sts; N3: 15 (16) sts.

Next rnd: N1: Work Rnd 1 of Hand chart; N2: work Rnd 1 of Hand chart over first st, place marker, work Rnd 1 of Thumb Gusset chart over next 5 sts, place marker, work in Hand chart over rem 24 (26) sts.

Work same as for left mitten.

Finishing
Block to finished measurements. ●

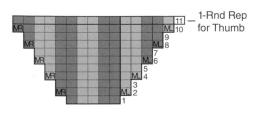

Celtic Moors
Thumb Gusset Chart

— 1-Rnd Rep
for Thumb

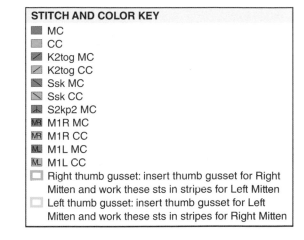

STITCH AND COLOR KEY
- MC
- CC
- K2tog MC
- K2tog CC
- Ssk MC
- Ssk CC
- S2kp2 MC
- M1R MC
- M1R CC
- M1L MC
- M1L CC
- Right thumb gusset: insert thumb gusset for Right Mitten and work these sts in stripes for Left Mitten
- Left thumb gusset: insert thumb gusset for Left Mitten and work these sts in stripes for Right Mitten

PALM   **CELTIC MOORS**

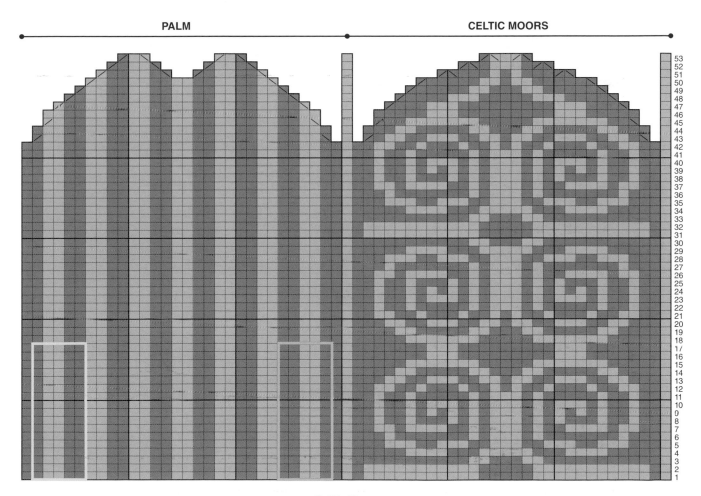

Celtic Moors
Size S/M Hand Chart

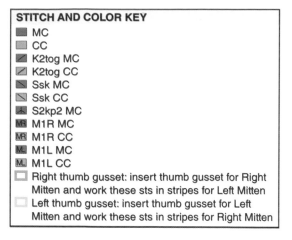

STITCH AND COLOR KEY
- ■ MC
- □ CC
- ◪ K2tog MC
- ◪ K2tog CC
- ◪ Ssk MC
- ◪ Ssk CC
- ⊥ S2kp2 MC
- M1R MC
- M1R CC
- M1L MC
- M1L CC
- ☐ Right thumb gusset: insert thumb gusset for Right Mitten and work these sts in stripes for Left Mitten
- ☐ Left thumb gusset: insert thumb gusset for Left Mitten and work these sts in stripes for Right Mitten

PALM   CELTIC MOORS

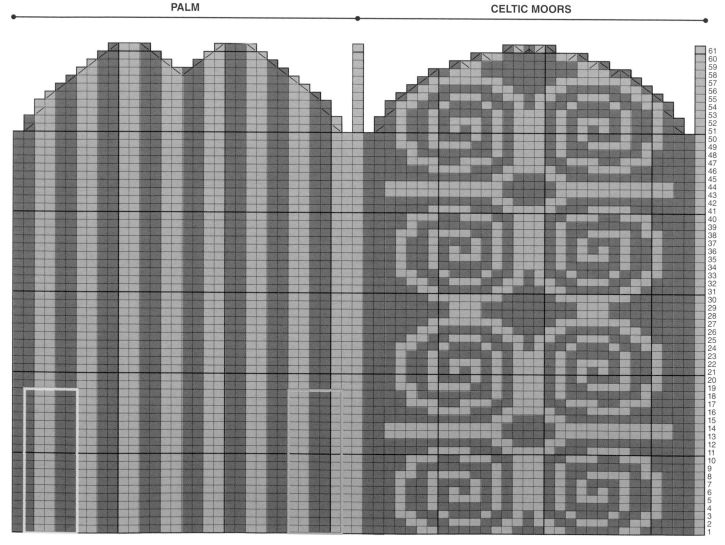

Celtic Moors
Size M/L Hand Chart

Provincial Garden

Adorn your hands with warmth and elegance wearing these embroidered beauties.

Design by Diane Zangl

Skill Level
■■■◻ INTERMEDIATE

Sizes
Adult small/medium (medium/large)
Instructions are given for the smaller size with larger size in parentheses. When only 1 number is listed, it applies to both sizes.

Finished Measurements
Hand circumference: 8 (9) inches
Length: 11 (11½) inches

Materials
- Berroco Peruvia worsted weight (100% Peruvian highland wool; 174 yds/100g per hank): 3 (3) hanks nougat #7128 (MC), small amounts of sea turtle #7125 (A), bing cherry #7151 (B), mostaza #7119 (C) and naraja #7110 (D) for embroidery
- Size 8 (5mm) double-point needles (set of 5) or size needed to obtain gauge
- Stitch holders
- Stitch markers

4 MEDIUM

Gauge
16 sts and 23 rnds = 4 inches/10cm in St st with 2 strands held tog.

To save time, take time to check gauge.

Special Abbreviation
N1, N2, N3: Needle 1, Needle 2, Needle 3

Pattern Note
Mittens are worked with 2 strands held together throughout. Embroidery is worked with 1 strand.

Right Mitten
With MC, cast on 28 (32) sts. Distribute sts evenly on 4 needles. Place marker for beg of rnd and join, taking care not to twist sts.

Knit 1 rnd, inc 4 sts evenly around—32 (36) sts.

Work even in St st until mitten measures 2½ inches from beg.

Thumb opening
Next rnd: K2, drop yarn, with short piece of waste yarn knit next 6 (7) sts, slip these sts back to LH needle and knit them again with MC, then knit to end.

Work even until mitten measures 6½ (7) inches from beg.

Shape top
Rnd 1: [K2, k2tog] around—24 (27) sts.

Rnd 2: Knit.

Rnd 3: [K2tog, k1] around—16 (18) sts.

Rnd 4: Knit.

Rnd 5: [K2tog] around—8 (9) sts.

Cut yarn and draw through rem sts.

Cuff
Pick up and knit 1 st in each purl bump behind each cast-on st—28 (32) sts. Place marker for beg of rnd and join.

Knit 1 rnd, inc 4 sts evenly around—32 (36) sts.

Working even in St st for 1 inch, inc 4 sts evenly on last rnd—36 (40) sts.

Working even for 1½ inches, inc 4 sts evenly on last rnd—40 (44) sts.

Work even for ½ inch.

Purl 2 rnds. Bind off pwise.

Thumb

Remove waste yarn and slip loops to 3 dpns. Distribute sts with 4 (5) sts on N1, 4 sts on N2 and 4 (5) sts on N3—12 (14) sts. Place marker for beg of rnd and join.

Work even in St st until thumb measures 2½ (2¾) inches, or desired length.

Shape top

Dec rnd: [K2tog] around—6 (7) sts.

Cut yarn and draw through rem sts.

Left Mitten

With MC, cast on 28 (32) sts. Distribute sts evenly on 4 needles. Place marker for beg of rnd and join, taking care not to twist sts.

Knit 1 rnd, inc 4 sts evenly around—32 (36) sts.

Work even in St st until mitten measures 2½ inches from beg.

Thumb opening

Next rnd: K8 (9), drop yarn, with short piece of waste yarn knit next 6 (7) sts, slip these sts back to LH needle and knit them again with MC, then knit to around to end.

Work hand and thumb same as for right mitten.

Finishing

Block to measurements.

Embroider cuff and back of hand following Fig. 1 on page 20. ●

Cuff

STITCH AND COLOR KEY
A
B
C
D

Lazy Daisy Stitch

Stem Stitch

Straight Stitch

Mitten Back

Figure 1

English Popovers

Chunky cables and bobbles accent these "special occasion" mittens.

Design by Diane Zangl

Skill Level
◼◼◼▢ INTERMEDIATE

Sizes
Woman's small/medium (medium/large) Instructions are given for smaller size, with larger size in parentheses. When only 1 number is given, it applies to both sizes.

Finished Measurements
Hand circumference: 6¾ (7¾) inches
Total length: 9 (10) inches

Materials
- Brown Sheep Lamb's Pride Bulky (bulky weight; 85% wool/15% mohair; 125 yds/100g per skein): 1 (2) skeins wild violet #M173
- Size 6 (4mm) double-point needles (set of 4) or size needed to obtain gauge
- Cable needle
- Stitch holders
- Stitch markers

Gauge
16 sts and 24 rnds = 4 inches/10cm in St st.

To save time, take time to check gauge.

Special Abbreviation
N1, N2, N3: Needle 1, Needle 2, Needle 3

Special Techniques
Make 1 Left (M1L): Insert LH needle from front to back under strand between the last st worked and the next st on LH needle, k1-tbl. Stitch slants to the left.

Make 1 Right (M1R): Insert LH needle from back to front under strand between the last st worked and the next st on LH needle, k1 through front of loop. Stitch slants to the right.

Pattern Stitch
Chart A

See chart. Read all rounds of chart from right to left.

Mock Cable (multiple of 3 sts)
Rnd 1: *K2, p1; rep from * around.
Rnd 2: *Knit 2nd st on LH needle through front of loop, knit first st, slip both sts off needle, p1; rep from * around.

Rep Rnds 1 and 2 for pat.

Left Mitten

Cuff
Cast on 27 (30) sts. Distribute sts evenly on 3 needles. Place marker for beg of rnd and join, taking care not to twist sts.

Work in Mock Cable pat until cuff measures 2½ inches, inc 2 (3) sts on last rnd—29 (33) sts.

Thumb gusset
Set up pat: K2, place marker, k1, place marker, k3, work Rnd 1 of Chart A over next 11 sts, knit to end of rnd.

Inc rnd: K2, slip maker, M1L, k1, M1R, slip marker, work in established pat to end of rnd—31 (35) sts. Continuing in established pat, inc 2 sts between markers [every other rnd] 4 (5) more times—39 (45) sts.

Hand
K2, sl 11 (13) sts between markers to holder for thumb, cast on 1, work to end of rnd—29 (33) sts. Work even in established pat until mitten measures 8 (9) inches from cast-on edge.

Shape top
Rnd 1: [K2tog, k1] 9 (11) times, [k2tog] 1 (0) time(s)—19 (22) sts.
Rnd 2: Knit around.
Rnd 3: K1, *k2tog, k1; rep from * around—13 (15) sts.
Rnd 4: Knit around.

Rnd 5: [K2tog] 6 (7) times, k1—7 (8) sts. Cut yarn and draw through rem sts.

Thumb

Slip sts from holder to 2 needles, pick up and knit 1 st in cast-on edge of opening—12 (14) sts. Distribute sts with 4 (5) sts on N1, 4 sts on N2 and 4 (5) sts on N3. Place marker for beg of rnd and join.
Work even in St st until thumb measures 2¼ (2¾) inches.

Shape thumb top

Dec rnd: [K2tog] around—6 (7) sts. Cut yarn and draw through rem sts.

Right Mitten

Cuff

Work same as for left cuff.

Thumb gusset

Set-up rnd: K12 (16), work Rnd 1 of Chart A over next 11 sts, k3, place marker, k1, place marker, k2.

Inc rnd: Work in established pat to last 3 sts, slip maker, M1L, k1, M1R, slip marker, k2—31 (35) sts. Continuing in established pat, inc 2 sts between markers [every other rnd] 4 (5) more times—39 (45) sts.

Hand

Work 26 (30) sts as established, sl 11 (13) sts between markers to holder for thumb, cast on 1, k2—29 (33) sts. Work remainder of mitten same as for left mitten. ●

English Popovers Mittens
Chart A

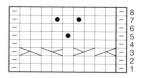

STITCH KEY
☐ Knit
⊟ Purl
⦿ Bobble: [K1, yo, k1, yo, k1] in same st, turn, p5, turn, pass 2nd, 3rd, 4th and 5th st over first, then knit in the back of this st.
⋈⋈ ⋈⋈ Cable: Sl 2 sts to cn and hold in back, k2, k2 from cn, k1, sl 2 sts to cn and hold in front, k2, k2 from cn.

Ruffles & Ribbons

These pretty mitts, worked back and forth, add excitement with central oval drop stitch styling.

Design by Kara Gott Warner

Skill Level
◗■□□ EASY

Size
One size fits most

Finished Measurements
Hand circumference: 7½ inches
Length: 8 inches

Materials
- Knit One, Crochet Too Brae Tweed (worsted weight; 60% merino wool/20% baby llama/10% bamboo/10% donegal; 109 yds/50g per skein): 2 skeins berry heather #261
- Size 7 (4.5mm) needles or size needed to obtain gauge
- 2 yds 1-inch-wide ribbon, (preferably with elastic or some stretch) in color of choice

Gauge
19 sts and 25 rows = 4 inches/10cm in St st.

To save time, take time to check gauge.

Special Technique
Yo twice: Wrap yarn twice around RH needle.

Pattern Notes
Mitts are worked back and forth in rows beginning at the ruffle and working to the top of mitt.

The seam is made at the side, leaving a 2-inch opening for the thumb.

Refer to Drop Stitch Techniques on page 47 for more information on working and dropping yarn over wraps.

Right Mitt

Ruffle
Cast on 72 sts. Work in St st until ruffle measures 2 inches, ending with a WS row.

Next row (RS): [K2tog] across—36 sts.

Next row: [K2, p2] across.

Rep last row until rib measures approx 1 inch, ending with a WS row.

Eyelet row (RS): *K2, yo, k2tog; rep from * across—36 sts.

Next row: Purl.

Work in St st until right mitt measures 4½ inches from beg, ending with a WS row.

Hand
Row 1 (RS): Knit.

Row 2: Purl.

Row 3: Knit.

Row 4: P21, k11, p4.

Row 5: K4, [k1, yo] 3 times, [k1, yo twice] 5 times, [k1, yo] 3 times, k21.

Row 6: P21, k11 dropping all yo's, p4.

Rep [Rows 1–6] twice more.

Work in St st until right mitt measures 8 inches from beg.

Bind off all sts.

Left Mitt

Ruffle
Work same as for right ruffle.

Hand

Row 1 (RS): Knit.

Row 2: Purl.

Row 3: Knit.

Row 4: P4, k11, p21.

Row 5: K21, [k1, yo] 3 times, [k1, yo twice] 5 times, [k1, yo] 3 times, k4.

Row 6: P4, k11 dropping all yo's, p21.

Rep [Rows 1–6] twice more.

Work in St st until mitt measures 8 inches from beg.

Bind off all sts.

Finishing

Fold mitt in half, and sew side seam starting from bound-off edge to approx 2 inches from top, leave a 2-inch opening for thumb, and then sew rest of seam closed.

Beg and ending at center of drop st pat, weave ribbon through eyelets and tie ends in bow.

Rep for other mitt.

Block lightly to finished measurements. ●

Lil' Bambinos

These flip-top mittens make playing peek-a-boo so much more fun!

Design by Moira Engel

Skill Level

■■■□ INTERMEDIATE

Sizes
Child's 4–6 (7–8, 10–12) Instructions are given for smallest size, with larger sizes in parentheses. When only 1 number is given, it applies to all sizes.

Finished Measurements
Hand circumference: 5¼ (6¼, 7) inches
Length: 6 (7½, 8½) inches, unbuttoned

Materials

- Wisdom Yarns Poems (worsted weight; 100% wool; 109 yds/50g per ball): 1 (1, 1) ball blue/orange/purple multi #583
- Size 7 (4.5mm) double-point needles (set of 5)
- Size 8 (5mm) double-point needles (set of 5) or size needed to obtain gauge
- Size G/6 (4mm) crochet hook
- Stitch markers
- 4 locking markers or safety pins
- Stitch holders
- 2 (¾-inch) buttons

Gauge
18 sts and 26 rows = 4 inches/10cm in St st with larger needles.

To save time, take time to check gauge.

Special Techniques
Loose Bind-Off: *K2tog-tbl, slip resulting st back to LH needle; rep from * until all sts are bound off.

Make 1 Left (M1L): Insert LH needle from front to back under strand between the last st worked and the next st on LH needle, k1-tbl. St slants to the left.

Make 1 Right (M1R): Insert LH needle from back to front under strand between the last st worked and the next st on LH needle, k1 through front of loop. St slants to the right.

Pattern Notes
When working with double-point needles for the first time, the cast-on may seem tricky. Try casting on all stitches onto one needle, then distribute them evenly over three or four needles as directed in the pattern, and arrange the needles so that the stitches are not twisted, then join. For more information on working on double-point needles, refer to page 4.

By using five double-point needles instead of four (you'll have stitches on four of the needles, with the fifth as your working needle), it's less likely that you'll get unsightly gaps between stitches when changing from one needle to the next.

To make mittens that approximately match, make sure to begin casting on at about the same spot in the color sequence for both mittens.

Left Mitten

Cuff
With smaller dpns, loosely cast on 24 (28, 32) sts. Distribute evenly on 4 needles. Place marker for beg of rnd and join, taking care not to twist sts.

Next rnd: [K2, p2] around.

Rep last rnd until rib measures 1½ (2, 2½) inches.

Change to larger dpns.

Knit 3 rnds.

Thumb gusset
Inc Rnd 1: K5 (6, 7), place marker, M1L, k1, M1R, place marker, k18 (21, 24)—26 (30, 34) sts.

Knit 1 rnd even.

Inc Rnd 2: K5 (6, 7), slip marker, M1L, knit to next gusset marker, M1R, slip marker, knit to end— 28 (32, 36) sts.

Knit 1 rnd even.

Rep [last 2 rnds] 2 (4, 5) more times—32 (40, 46) sts.

Hand

K5 (6, 7), remove marker, slip next 9 (13, 15) sts on holder for thumb, cast on 1, remove marker, knit to end—24 (28, 32) sts.

Knit 2 (3, 3) rnds even.

Next rnd: K7 (8, 9), place locking marker on last st worked, k10 (12, 14), place locking marker on last st worked, knit to end.

Change to smaller dpns.

Next rnd: [K2, p2] around.

Rep [last rnd] 2 (2, 3) more times. Bind off using Loose Bind-Off.

Top flap

With larger dpns and holding yarn inside hand at WS, beg at marked st above thumb gusset, pick up and knit 1 st in each st to 2nd marked st along last rnd before rib—12 (14, 16) sts. Cut yarn, leaving a tail to weave in.

Cast on 6 (7, 8) sts, knit 12 (14, 16) picked up sts, cast on 6 (7, 8) sts—24 (28, 32) sts.

Place marker for beg of rnd and join, taking care not to twist sts.

Next rnd: K2, p2, k2, p0 (1, 2), k12 (15, 18), p2, k2, p2.

Rep [last rnd] 2 (2, 3) more times.

Work in St st until piece measures approx 5¼ (6½, 7) inches from beg, end last rnd at side of hand. Remove previous beg of rnd marker and place markers at new beg of rnd and after 12 (14, 16) sts.

Shape top

Dec Rnd: *K1, k2tog, knit to 3 sts before next side marker, k2tog, k1; rep from * once more—20 (24, 28) sts.

Knit 1 rnd even.

Rep [last 2 rnds] 2 (3, 4) more times—12 sts.

Place 6 sts on one needle and 6 on another needle and graft top using Kitchener stitch (see page 43).

Thumb

Slip sts from holders to larger dpns—9 (13, 15) sts. Distribute evenly on 3 needles. Place marker for beg of rnd and join.

Work even in St st until thumb measures approx 1½ (1¾, 2) inches.

Shape top

Dec rnd: [K2tog] 4 (6, 7) times, k1—5 (7, 8) sts.

Knit 1 rnd even.

Next rnd: [K2tog] 0 (3, 4) times, k0, (1, 0)—
5 (4, 4) sts.

Cut yarn and draw through rem sts.

Right Mitten
Work same as left mitten for cuff, thumb gusset
and hand.

Top flap
With larger dpns and holding yarn inside hand at WS,
beg at marked st on side of hand opposite thumb
gusset and, pick up and knit 1 st in each st to 2nd
marked st along last rnd before rib—12 (14, 16) sts.

Cut yarn, leaving a tail to weave in.

Work same as left mitten for rem of top flap
and thumb.

Finishing
Block to finished measurements.

Button loop
With crochet hook, join yarn in top edge of flap at
Kitchener stitch join with a sl st, ch 5, sc in top edge
of flap on opposite side of join. Fasten off.

Sew button to top of hand as pictured. ●

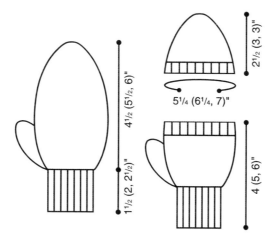

Lil' Bambinos Mittens Diagram

Erin Isle

This intermediate mitten uses a simple Fair Isle chart, making it a perfect first-time color-work project.

Design by Lisa Ellis

. . . .

Skill Level

■■ ■■ ■■ ▢ INTERMEDIATE

Sizes

Child's 4–6 (woman's small/medium)
Instructions are given for smaller size, with larger size in parentheses. When only 1 number is given, it applies to both sizes.

Finished Measurements

Hand circumference: 6½ (7¾) inches
Length: 9½ (12½) inches

Materials

- Cascade Yarns 220 Superwash (worsted weight; 100% superwash wool; 220 yds/100g per ball): 1 ball each teal #811 (MC), green #891 (A) and orange #876 (B)
- Size 5 (3.75mm) 40-inch circular needle
- Size 6 (4mm) 40-inch circular needle or size needed to obtain gauge
- Stitch markers

4 MEDIUM

Gauge

22 sts and 32 rows = 4 inches/10cm in St st with larger needle.

To save time, take time to check gauge.

Special Abbreviations

Make 1 (M1): Increase by making a backward loop over RH needle.

Make 1 Left (M1L): Insert LH needle from front to back under strand between the last st worked and the next st on LH needle, k1-tbl. St slants to the left.

Make 1 Right (M1R): Insert LH needle from back to front under strand between last st worked and next st on LH needle, k1 through front of loop. St slants to the right.

MLN1, MLN2: Magic Loop Needle 1, Magic Loop Needle 2.

Pattern Stitch

See chart. Read all rnds of chart from right to left.

Pattern Notes

Mitten is worked from the cuff up using the Magic Loop technique. For more information on using the Magic Loop method, refer to page 6.

An extra long ribbed cuff is worked to allow for it to be folded up.

Left Mitten

Cuff

With smaller needle and MC, cast on 36 (42) sts. Distribute evenly on each MLN. Place marker for beg of rnd and join, taking care not to twist sts.

Work in k1, p1 rib for 3 (4) inches.

Change to larger needle. Knit 1 rnd.

Work Rnds 1–8 of Chart 1.

Next rnd: With MC, knit.

Thumb gusset

Set-up rnd: M1, knit to end—37 (43) sts; 19 (22) st on MLN1 and 18 (21) sts on MLN2.

Inc rnd: MLN1: K18 (21) sts, place marker, M1L, k1; MLN2: M1R, place marker, k18 (21) sts—39 (45) sts.

Knit 2 rnds even.

Rep [last 3 rnds] 5 (7) more times—49 (59) sts.

Next rnd: Knit to first marker, place next 13 (17) sts onto waste yarn for thumb, M1, knit to end—37 (43) sts.

Hand

Work in St st until mitten measures 5 (7) inches from top of rib, or approx 1½ inches less than desired length.

Next rnd: K1, ssk, knit to end—36 (42) sts; 18 (21) sts on each needle.

Shape top

Dec rnd: MLN1: K1, ssk, knit to last 2 sts on needle, k2tog; MLN2: work same as MLN1—32 (38) sts.

Rep dec rnd [every other rnd] 3 (4) more times, then [every rnd] 2 (1) time(s)—12 (18) sts; 6 (9) sts rem on each MLN.

Graft top using Kitchener stitch, page 43.

Thumb

Place sts from waste yarn onto larger needle. Distribute sts with 7 (9) sts on MLN1 and 6 (8) sts on MLN2.

With MC, knit across row, M1—14 (18) sts; 7 (9) sts on each MLN. Place marker for beg of rnd and join.

Work in St st until thumb measures 1 (1½) inch(es) or desired length.

Shape top

Rnd 1: [K2, k2tog] around to last 2 sts, k2—11 (14) sts. Distribute sts evenly on needles as necessary.

Rnd 2: K1 (0), [k2tog] around—6 (7) sts.

Cut yarn and thread through rem sts.

Right Mitten

Work same as for left mitten.

Finishing

Block to finished measurements. •

8
7
6
5
4
3
2
1

6-st rep

COLOR KEY
MC
A
B

Erin Isle
Chart

Bollicina

Free-floating intarsia bubbles paired with Fair Isle polka dots make these children's mittens eye-catching and interesting to knit.

Design by Amy Marshall

Skill Level

◼◼◼◻ INTERMEDIATE

Sizes
Child's 6–8 (8–10) Instructions are given for smaller size, with larger size in parentheses. When only 1 number is given, it applies to both sizes.

Finished Measurements
Hand circumference: 6½ (7½) inches
Length: 8 (10) inches

Materials
- Jil Eaton Minnow Merino (worsted weight; 100% extra fine merino; 77 yds/50g per skein): 1 skein each orangini #4785 (MC), pinque #4789 (A) and icy pinque #4719 (B)
- Size 7 (4.5mm) double-point needles (set of 4)
- Size 8 (5mm) double-point needles (set of 4) or size needed to obtain gauge
- Stitch markers
- Stitch holder
- Bobbins (optional)
- Tapestry needle

4 MEDIUM

Gauge
16 sts and 25 rows = 4 inches/10cm in St st with larger needles.

To save time, take time to check gauge.

Pattern Notes
Pattern is worked from a chart using intarsia method. Refer to Intarsia Techniques on page 45 for more information on working with multiple colors and bobbins. Prepare a bobbin for each color area, allowing ¾ inch of yarn for each stitch plus 10 inches extra to weave in later.

To knit intarsia in the round, it is necessary to purl every other row, just as you would if you were knitting back and forth, turning at the last color change. It is also necessary to twist the yarns before you begin the next row and when changing colors to avoid creating holes in your work. When increasing or decreasing stitches in a pattern area, slip the first stitch of the shape as necessary.

Use stitch markers in two colors: Three of one color to mark the sides of the mittens and thumb gusset, and two of another color to mark sides of the intarsia pattern.

Right Mitten

Cuff
With smaller needles and A, cast on 28 (32) sts.

Distribute sts evenly on 3 needles. Place marker for beg of rnd and join, being careful not to twist sts.

Knit 6 rnds.

Change to MC. Knit 1 rnd.

Work Rnds 1–9 of Chart 1.

Change to larger needles.

Next rnd: Knit, placing markers as follows: k1 (2), place marker for intarsia pat, k11 (12), place marker for thumb gusset, k1 (0), place marker for intarsia pat, k2 (4), place marker for thumb gusset, knit to end of rnd.

Thumb gusset
Note: *Beg Chart 2 after the first (4th) rnd of the thumb gusset.*

Inc rnd: Knit to first thumb gusset marker, M1L, knit to next thumb gusset marker, M1R, knit to end of rnd—30 (34) sts.

Rep inc rnd [every 3 rnds] 2 (3) times more—34 (40) sts.

Hand

Next rnd: Work as established to first thumb gusset marker, remove marker, k1, cast on 5 (6) sts, sl 7 (10) sts to st holder, knit to end, removing 2nd thumb gusset marker—32 (36) sts.

Work 2 rnds even.

Dec rnd: Work 14 (15) sts as established, place marker for side of mitten, ssk, k1 (2), k2tog, knit to end of rnd—30 (34) sts.

Work 2 rnds even.

Dec rnd size 6–8: Work 14 sts as established, sk2p, knit to end of rnd—28 sts.

Dec rnd size 8–10: Work 15 sts as established, ssk, k2tog, knit to end of rnd—32 sts.

Both sizes: Work 9 (16) rnds even.

Shape top

Rnd 1: *K1, ssk, work to 3 sts before side marker, k2tog, k1; rep from * once more—24 (28) sts.

Work 1 rnd even.

Rep [last 2 rnds] 4 (5) times more—8 sts.

Place 4 sts on one needle and 4 on another needle and graft top using Kitchener stitch, page 43.

Thumb

Pick up and knit 1 st at side of thumb opening,
5 (6) sts across cast-on edge, 1 st on other side of thumb opening, knit across 7 (10) sts from holder—14 (18) sts. Place marker for beg of rnd and join to work in rnds.

Distribute sts evenly on 3 needles.

Dec rnd: K1, ssk, k1, k2tog, knit to end—12 (16) sts.

Knit 1 rnd even.

Dec rnd size 6–8: K1, sk2p, knit to end—10 sts.

Dec rnd size 8–10: K1, ssk, k2tog, knit to end—14 sts.

Knit 6 (9) rnds even.

Cut yarn and thread through rem sts.

Left Mitten

Work same as for right mitten to end of Chart 1.

Change to larger needles.

Knit 1 rnd placing markers as follows: place marker for side of mitten, k12 (14), place marker for thumb gusset, k3 (4), place marker for thumb gusset, k0 (1), place marker for intarsia pat, k12, place marker for intarsia pat, k1 (2).

Thumb gusset
Note: *Beg Chart 3 after the first (4th) rnd of the thumb gusset.*

Inc rnd: Knit to first thumb gusset marker, M1L, knit to next thumb gusset marker, M1R, knit to end of rnd—30 (34) sts.

Work 2 rnds even.

Rep [last 3 rnds] 2 (3) times more—34 (40) sts.

Hand & Thumb
Work same as for left mitten.

Finishing
Block to finished measurements.

Referring to photo, thread tapestry needle, and work stem stitch (also known as crewel stitch) as follows:

Step 1: Working from left to right, bring the thread up from the back of the work, to the point that you want to begin the stitch.

Step 2: Bring the needle up, a little to the back of the first stitch.

Step 3: Pull the thread through the work. Make the second stitch by bringing the needle out a little to the back of the second stitch.

Repeat Steps 1-3. ●

COLOR KEY
- MC
- A
- B

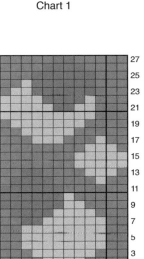

Bollicina
Chart 1

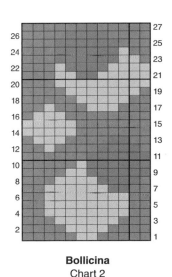

Bollicina
Chart 2

Bollicina
Chart 3

General Information

Abbreviations & Symbols

[ ] work instructions within brackets as many times as directed

( ) work instructions within parentheses in the place directed

** repeat instructions following the asterisks as directed

* repeat instructions following the single asterisk as directed

" inch(es)

approx approximately
beg begin/beginning
CC contrasting color
ch chain stitch
cm centimeter(s)
cn cable needle
dec decrease/decreases/ decreasing
dpn(s) double-pointed needle(s)
g gram
inc increase/increases/increasing

k knit
k2tog knit 2 stitches together
LH left hand
lp(s) loop(s)
m meter(s)
M1 make one stitch
MC main color
mm millimeter(s)
oz ounce(s)
p purl
pat(s) pattern(s)
p2tog purl 2 stitches together
psso pass slipped stitch over
p2sso pass 2 slipped stitches over
rem remain/remaining
rep repeat(s)
rev St st reverse stockinette stitch
RH right hand
rnd(s) rounds
RS right side
skp slip, knit, pass stitch over— one stitch decreased

sk2p slip 1, knit 2 together, pass slip stitch over the knit 2 together—2 stitches have been decreased
sl slip
sl 1k slip 1 knitwise
sl 1p slip 1 purlwise
sl st slip stitch(es)
ssk slip, slip, knit these 2 stitches together—a decrease
st(s) stitch(es)
St st stockinette stitch/stocking stitch
tbl through back loop(s)
tog together
WS wrong side
wyib with yarn in back
wyif with yarn in front
yd(s) yard(s)
yfwd yarn forward
yo yarn over

Skill Levels

BEGINNER

Beginner projects for first-time knitters using basic stitches. Minimal shaping.

EASY

Easy projects using basic stitches, repetitive stitch patterns, simple color changes and simple shaping and finishing.

INTERMEDIATE

Intermediate projects with a variety of stitches, mid-level shaping and finishing.

EXPERIENCED

Experienced projects using advanced techniques and stitches, detailed shaping and refined finishing.

Embroidery Stitches

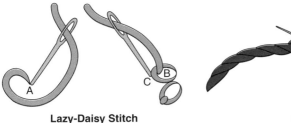

Lazy-Daisy Stitch

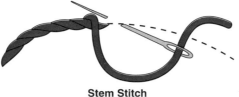

Stem Stitch

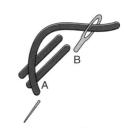

Straight Stitch

Standard Yarn Weight System
Categories of yarn, gauge ranges, and recommended needle sizes

Yarn Weight Symbol & Category Names	1 SUPER FINE	2 FINE	3 LIGHT	4 MEDIUM	5 BULKY	6 SUPER BULKY
Type of Yarns in Category	Sock, Fingering, Baby	Sport, Baby	DK, Light Worsted	Worsted, Afghan, Aran	Chunky, Craft, Rug	Bulky, Roving
Knit Gauge Range* in Stockinette Stitch to 4 inches	27–32 sts	23–26 sts	21–24 sts	16–20 sts	12–15 sts	6–11 sts
Recommended Needle in Metric Size Range	2.25–3.25mm	3.25–3.75mm	3.75–4.5mm	4.5–5.5mm	5.5–8mm	8mm and larger
Recommended Needle U.S. Size Range	1 to 3	3 to 5	5 to 7	7 to 9	9 to 11	11 and larger

* GUIDELINES ONLY: The above reflect the most commonly used gauges and needle sizes for specific yarn categories.

Inches Into Millimeters & Centimeters
All measurements are rounded off slightly.

inches	mm	cm	inches	cm	inches	cm	inches	cm
⅛	3	0.3	5	12.5	21	53.5	38	96.5
¼	6	0.6	5½	14	22	56.0	39	99.0
⅜	10	1.0	6	15.0	23	58.5	40	101.5
½	13	1.3	7	18.0	24	61.0	41	104.0
⅝	15	1.5	8	20.5	25	63.5	42	106.5
¾	20	2.0	9	23.0	26	66.0	43	109.0
⅞	22	2.2	10	25.5	27	68.5	44	112.0
1	25	2.5	11	28.0	28	71.0	45	114.5
1¼	32	3.2	12	30.5	29	73.5	46	117.0
1½	38	3.8	13	33.0	30	76.0	47	119.5
1¾	45	4.5	14	35.5	31	79.0	48	122.0
2	50	5.0	15	38.0	32	81.5	49	124.5
2½	65	6.5	16	40.5	33	84.0	50	127.0
3	75	7.5	17	43.0	34	86.5		
3½	90	9.0	18	46.0	35	89.0		
4	100	10.0	19	48.5	36	91.5		
4½	115	11.5	20	51.0	37	94.0		

Knitting Basics

. . . .

Cast-On

Leaving an end about an inch long for each stitch to be cast on, make a slip knot on the right needle.

Place the thumb and index finger of your left hand between the yarn ends with the long yarn end over your thumb, and the strand from the skein over your index finger. Close your other fingers over the strands to hold them against your palm. Spread your thumb and index fingers apart and draw the yarn into a "V."

Place the needle in front of the strand around your thumb and bring it underneath this strand. Carry the needle over and under the strand on your index finger.

Draw through loop on thumb.

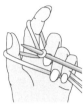

Drop the loop from your thumb and draw up the strand to form a stitch on the needle.

Repeat until you have cast on the number of stitches indicated in the pattern. Remember to count the beginning slip knot as a stitch.

Cable Cast-On

This type of cast-on is used when adding stitches in the middle or at the end of a row.

Make a slip knot on the left needle. Knit a stitch in this knot and place it on the left needle. Insert the right needle between the last two stitches on the left needle. Knit a stitch and place it on the left needle. Repeat for each stitch needed.

Knit (k)

Insert tip of right needle from front to back in next stitch on left needle.

Bring yarn under and over the tip of the right needle.

Pull yarn loop through the stitch with right needle point.

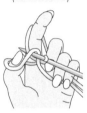

Slide the stitch off the left needle. The new stitch is on the right needle.

Purl (p)

With yarn in front, insert tip of right needle from back to front through next stitch on the left needle.

Bring yarn around the right needle counterclockwise.

With right needle, draw yarn back through the stitch.

Slide the stitch off the left needle. The new stitch is on the right needle.

Bind-Off

Binding off (knit)

Knit first two stitches on left needle. Insert tip of left needle into first stitch worked on right needle and pull it over the second stitch and completely off the needle.

Knit the next stitch and repeat. When one stitch remains on right needle, cut yarn and draw tail through last stitch to fasten off.

Binding off (purl)

Purl first two stitches on left needle. Insert tip of left needle into first stitch worked on right needle and pull it over the second stitch and completely off the needle.

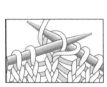

Purl the next stitch and repeat. When one stitch remains on right needle, cut yarn and draw tail through last stitch to fasten off.

Increase (inc)

Two stitches in one stitch

Increase (knit)

Knit the next stitch in the usual manner, but don't remove the stitch from the left needle. Place right needle behind left needle and knit again into the back of the same stitch. Slip original stitch off left needle.

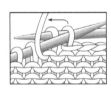

Increase (purl)

Purl the next stitch in the usual manner, but don't remove the stitch from the left needle. Place right needle behind left needle and purl again into the back of the same stitch. Slip original stitch off left needle.

Invisible Increase (M1)
There are several ways to make or increase one stitch.

Make 1 with Left Twist (M1L)
Insert left needle from front to back under the horizontal loop between the last stitch worked and next stitch on left needle.

With right needle, knit into the back of this loop.

To make this increase on the purl side, insert left needle in same manner and purl into the back of the loop.

Make 1 with Right Twist (M1R)
Insert left needle from back to front under the horizontal loop between the last stitch worked and next stitch on left needle.

With right needle, knit into the front of this loop.

To make this increase on the purl side, insert left needle in same manner and purl into the front of the loop.

Make 1 with Backward Loop over the right needle
With your thumb, make a loop over the right needle.

Slip the loop from your thumb onto the needle and pull to tighten.

Make 1 in top of stitch below
Insert tip of right needle into the stitch on left needle one row below.

Knit this stitch, then knit the stitch on the left needle.

Decrease (dec)

Knit 2 together (k2tog)
Put tip of right needle through next two stitches on left needle as to knit. Knit these two stitches as one.

Purl 2 together (p2tog)
Put tip of right needle through next two stitches on left needle as to purl. Purl these two stitches as one.

Slip, Slip, Knit (ssk)
Slip next two stitches, one at a time, as to knit from left needle to right needle.

Insert left needle in front of both stitches and work off needle together.

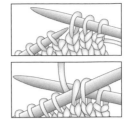
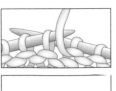

Slip, Slip, Purl (ssp)
Slip next two stitches, one at a time, as to knit from left needle to right needle. Slip these stitches back onto left needle keeping them twisted. Purl these two stitches together through back loops.

Kitchener Stitch
This method of weaving with two needles is used for the toes of socks and flat seams. To weave the edges together and form an unbroken line of stockinette stitch, divide all stitches evenly onto two knitting needles—one behind the other. Thread yarn into tapestry needle. Hold needles with wrong sides together and work from right to left as follows:

Step 1: Insert tapestry needle into first stitch on front needle as to purl. Draw yarn through stitch, leaving stitch on knitting needle.

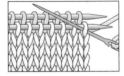

Step 2: Insert tapestry needle into the first stitch on the back needle as to purl. Draw yarn through stitch and slip stitch off knitting needle.

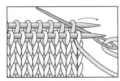

Step 3: Insert tapestry needle into the next stitch on same (back) needle as to knit, leaving stitch on knitting needle.

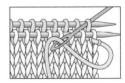

Step 4: Insert tapestry needle into the first stitch on the front needle as to knit. Draw yarn through stitch and slip stitch off knitting needle.

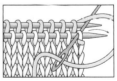

Step 5: Insert tapestry needle into the next stitch on same (front) needle as to purl. Draw yarn through stitch, leaving stitch on knitting needle.

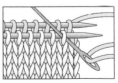

Repeat Steps 2 through 5 until one stitch is left on each needle. Then repeat Steps 2 and 4. Fasten off. Woven stitches should be the same size as adjacent knitted stitches.

Stitch & Color Techniques

. . . .

Working from Charts

When working with more than one color in a row or round, sometimes a chart is provided to follow the pattern. On the chart each square represents one stitch. A key is given indicating the color or stitch represended by each color or symbol in the box.

When working in rows, right-side rows are read from right to left, and wrong-side rows are read from left to right.

When working in rounds, every row on the chart is a right-side row and is read from right to left. The placement of the number on the chart indicate the beginning of the row or round.

Stranded or Fair Isle Knitting

Changing colors of yarn within the round or row is called Stranded or Fair Isle knitting, and is most commonly worked in the round. This type of knitting can be worked either with both yarns in one hand, as shown in the photo to the right, or with one yarn in each hand. Carry the yarns along the wrong side of the fabric, working each color in the order indicated by the pattern. One color should always be carried under the other, whether you are knitting or purling—the strands will run parallel on the wrong side, as shown below. They should never change positions; if they do, it will be apparent on the right side of the fabric. If working back and forth, carry

both yarns to the end of each row and twist to "lock" them in position on the last stitch. When working in the round, there is no need to twist the yarns at the end of every round.

When one of the yarns is carried across the back for more than 5 stitches (or about an inch), the yarn

should be caught into the back of one of the stitches that is worked with the other yarn. This will prevent snags caused by long floats.

Fair Isle knitting creates a denser fabric than plain Stockinette knitting. Always work your gauge swatch in pattern before beginning your project. Watch your tension, ensuring that the stranded yarn is not pulled too tight; this will create puckers on the front of the fabric.

Intarsia

In certain patterns there are larger areas of color within the piece. Since this type of pattern requires a new color only for that section, it is not necessary to carry the yarn back and forth across the back. For this type of color change, a separate ball of yarn or bobbin is used for each section of color, making the yarn available only where needed.

Before beginning the project wind a bobbin for each color area, allowing ¾ inch for each stitch plus 10 inches extra to weave in at beginning and end of color section.

Bring the new yarn being used up and around the yarn just worked; this will twist, or "lock" the colors and prevent holes from occurring at the join. The two bottom photos show how the two colors are twisted together on the wrong side of the work.

Twined Knitting

Changing strands of yarn every stitch is called Twined Knitting or Tvåändsstickning. This method of knitting can be worked with either one or two colors and is done with both yarns held in the same hand. The strands can be carried across the back or front of the fabric, or changed from back to front, or vice versa, as needed for the pattern.

This method should be worked using center pull balls. If using two colors, use the strand coming from the center of each ball, and if using one color, use both the strand coming from the center of the ball and strand from the outside of the ball.

To work Twined Knitting, both strands are attached to the beginning of the round. Knit the first stitch with Strand 1. Bring Strand 2 up and over Strand 1 and knit the next stitch. Bring Strand 1 up and over Strand 2 and knit the next stitch. Repeat these last two steps, as shown to the right, until all the stitches have been worked, making sure to always change colors the same way across the round. Alternating two strands in this way, produces a nice neat twist, which can be seen from the wrong side of the work as shown below.

You'll notice after working the first round that the yarns have become very twisted. Untwisting them every round will make working each round much easier. To untwist the yarns when using two colors, simply pick up a ball of yarn in each hand, holding onto the end coming out of the center so no more comes out as you untwist the strands, and hold both balls so that the work on the needles dangles in the air. It will spin and untwist the strands. You can lower

the piece to a flat surface to slow it down as it nears the end to prevent the strands from retwisting in the other direction.

To untwist the strands when working from one ball of yarn, insert a double-point needle into the ball of yarn and tie a half-hitch over the needle using both strands (think of it as a backward loop cast-on stitch). Pick up the work on the needles, and allow the ball of yarn to dangle in the air. Allow it to spin and untwist the strands.

Twined Knitting produces a thick fabric that can be very dense and stiff depending on the yarn used and your knitting tension.

Yarn Over Drop Stitch

Step 1: Work to indicated position of yarn over, wrap yarn over once or twice as shown below.

Step 2: Work to the yarn overs and drop them off the needle to create an elongated stitch as shown in the photo below.

HOUSE of WHITE BIRCHES
PUBLISHERS SINCE 1947

Warm Hands Warm the Heart is published by DRG, 306 East Parr Road, Berne, IN 46711. Printed in USA. Copyright © 2010 DRG. All rights reserved. This publication may not be reproduced in part or in whole without written permission from the publisher.

RETAIL STORES: If you would like to carry this pattern book or any other DRG publications, visit DRGwholesale.com.

Every effort has been made to ensure that the instructions in this pattern book are complete and accurate. We cannot, however, take responsibility for human error, typographical mistakes or variations in individual work. Please visit AnniesAtticCustomerCare.com to check for pattern updates.

ISBN: 978-1-59217-319-8

1 2 3 4 5 6 7 8 9

Photo Index

8

17

21

12

24

27

32

36